A to Z Canada

BY TAMRA ORR

children's press®

A Division of Scholastic Inc.

New York Toronto London Auckland Sydney
Mexico City New Delhi Hong Kong
Danbury, Connecticut

Consultant: Dr. Allan K. McDougall, University of Western Ontario
Series Design: Marie O'Neill
Photo Research: Caroline Anderson

The photos on the cover show a polar bear (top left), the Hotel Frontenac (top right), a maple leaf (bottom right), and a young Canadian girl holding a maple leaf (bottom center).

Photographs © 2005: Bryan and Cherry Alexander Photography: 17 right, 18, 24, 33, 35 top; Corbis Images: 7 left (Tibor Bognár), 9 top (Jan Butchofsky-Houser), cover top left (John Conrad), 17 left (Natalie Fobes), 27 right, 32 (Raymond Gehman), 28 bottom (Lowell Georgia), 15 right (Dave G. Houser), 27 left (Wolfgang Kaehler), 19 (Kit Kittle), 7 right, 25 top (Gunter Marx Photography), 10 (Sally A. Morgan/Ecoscene), 34 bottom, 36 (Richard T. Nowitz), 16, 25 bottom (Carl & Ann Purcell), 29 (Paul A. Souders), cover center bottom, 6 top (Ron Watts), 37 top (Jim Young); Digital Vision/Mimotito: 5 bottom; Envision Stock Photography Inc./Deborah Burke: 11; Getty Images: 14 (Carlo Allegri), 37 bottom (Gary Cralle/The Image Bank), 8 (Andre Gallant/The Image Bank), 12 top (Photodisc Blue), cover bottom right (Siede Preis/Photodisc Green); Index Stock Imagery/HIRB: 28 top; Minden Pictures/Michael Quinton: 4; National Geographic Image Collection/K. Yamashita/PanStock/Panoramic Images: 34 top; Peter Arnold Inc./Klein: 5 top; Peter Langer Associated Media Group: 9 bottom; Photo Researchers, NY: 35 bottom (Ray Coleman), 23 (George Gerster); PhotoEdit/Elizabeth Zuckerman: 38; PictureQuest: 26 (Burke/Triolo/Brand X Pictures), 22 (Corbis), 21 (Creatas); Retna Ltd/Joseph Marzullo: 15 left; Robert Fried Photography: cover top right; Robertstock.com/George Hunter: 6 bottom, 30, 31; The Image Works/Topham: 12 bottom; The Public Archives of Canada: 13.
Map by XNR Productions, Inc.

Library of Congress Cataloging-in-Publication Data
Orr, Tamra.
  Canada / by Tamra Orr.
     p. cm. — (A to Z)
  Includes bibliographical references and index.
  ISBN 0-516-23661-X (lib. bdg.)   0-516-24950-9 (pbk.)
  1. Canada—Juvenile literature. I. Title. II. Series.
  F1008.2.O77 2005
  971—dc22   2005006994

1 2 3 4 5 6 7 8 9 10 R 14 13 12 11 10 09 08 07 06 05

▪ Contents

Animals

Beavers are busy throughout much of Canada.

The beaver has been a symbol for Canada since the 1600s. Beavers cut down trees with their strong teeth and build dams across many streams in Canada's forests. They are often thought of as the world's first engineers.

![Polar bear relaxing]

Polar bear relaxing

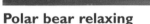

Puffins are black and white seabirds with colorful bills. One of the largest populations of puffins in the world is found on an island near Saint John's, Newfoundland. Bird-watchers often travel on ferries to look at these unusual creatures.

Atlantic puffins

Churchill, Manitoba, bills itself as the Polar Bear Capital of the World. Polar bears spend the summer on the shores of Hudson Bay. In winter, they live on the ice, where they catch fish and seals and give birth to their cubs.

A type of deer called caribou live in the **tundra** and northern forests. They travel in herds and eat mosses and **lichens**.

In spring and autumn, the skies are filled with the sights and sounds of Canada geese. In spring, these birds **migrate** to northern nesting grounds. In the fall, they fly south to warmer regions.

Quebec City, historic and modern

CN Tower in Toronto

Buildings

The world's tallest freestanding building is located in Toronto, Canada. The CN Tower (short for Canadian National Tower) stands 1,815 feet (553 meters) tall. Visitors can go to the top in a speedy glass elevator. The CN Tower has a restaurant, theater, and nightclub.

The Chateau Frontenac overlooks Quebec City and the Saint Lawrence River. This luxury hotel was built more than one hundred years ago.

Montreal at twilight

Scenic Vancouver is near both mountains and the ocean.

Cities

Toronto has more than 4 million people and is Canada's largest city. Montreal has more than 3 million people and is Canada's second-largest city. Montreal is also the world's second-largest French-speaking city, after Paris.

On the west coast, Vancouver is home to almost 2 million people, making it Canada's third-largest city. It is Canada's busiest port.

Quebec City is Canada's oldest city. It was founded in 1608 by the French explorer Samuel de Champlain.

Dress

Most Canadians wear contemporary clothes. They dress to be comfortable and wear warm pants, skirts, and sweaters when the weather is cold, and lighter-weight shirts, shorts, and dresses when it's warm.

An Edmonton family enjoys a bike ride.

In Nova Scotia, or "New Scotland," people of Scottish descent put on **kilts** for special occasions. In Vancouver's Chinatown, many Asians wear **kimonos**.

Some of the Inuit of the far north honor their heritage by wearing traditional seal fur coats and hats.

A kilt and bagpipes are signs of Scottish heritage.

This Inuit girl is wearing traditional seal skins.

Pulp and paper mill

Exports

With its vast forestland, Canada is one of the world's biggest timber exporters. Some wood is used for lumber. The rest is sent to pulp mills. There it is turned into paper and will eventually be used for books, magazines, and newspapers.

Canada exports a great deal of oil and fuel, as well. It also produces a lot of transportation equipment such as cars, trucks, airplanes, and subway cars.

Fiddlehead Fern Soup

WHAT YOU NEED:
- 4 cups fiddleheads
- 2 tablespoons unsalted butter
- 1 small onion
- 2 cups chicken stock
- 2 cups milk or cream
- 1/2 teaspoon lemon zest
- Salt and pepper to taste

HOW TO MAKE IT:
Bring a large pot of salted water to a boil. Add fiddleheads. Return to a boil and cook five to eight minutes. Drain and rinse with cold water. Chop and put aside. Melt butter in a saucepan. Add onion and cook for five minutes. Add fiddleheads and chicken stock. Stir, increase heat, and bring to a boil again. Cover and cook for five minutes. Add milk, reduce heat, and stir in the lemon zest. Season with salt and pepper.

Food

Maple syrup is a special treat in Canada. During the spring, the sap is gathered from maple trees and boiled until it turns into syrup. This process is called sugaring.

Fiddlehead ferns are another Canadian favorite. Edible fiddleheads are the young shoots of the ostrich fern. They taste a little like spinach. Ask an adult to help you make this recipe.

Parliament building
in Ottawa

Government

For many years, Great Britain governed Canada. Today, the Queen of England is also the Queen of Canada. The **monarch** is the official head of state in Canada. But Canada's monarch has little power. Canada is governed by a prime minister and a national parliament made up of an elected House of Commons and an appointed Senate.

The prime minister is usually the leader of the party with the most seats in the House. Canada's ten **provinces** have constitutional authority to govern themselves. Canada's three **territories** have some authority to govern themselves.

Canada's national police force is the Royal Canadian Mounted Police or "Mounties." On special occasions, they wear bright red uniforms, tan hats, and brown boots. Once they all rode horses, but now they drive police cars.

Mounties in parade formation

Bienvenue du Canada

(bee-YEN-vi-NU du can-a-DA)
means "Welcome to Canada!"
in French.

History

French explorer and fur trader Samuel de Champlain

In 1608, Samuel de Champlain founded a small colony on the Saint Lawrence River. He named the area Quebec. Other colonies sprang up as more French fur trappers and settlers came to Canada. But England was also interested in exploring and trading in this new land.

For many years, the French and the British fought over who should be in charge of the area. Finally in 1763, Great Britain won control of all the territories that had once been New France.

Today, French is still the official language of Quebec. Many of the people who live in the provinces of New Brunswick and Ontario also speak the language. Canadians who speak French are called francophones.

Popular singer Celine Dion was born in Quebec.

Important People

Canada is the home of many fine writers and musicians.

The birthplace of L. M. Montgomery

Children everywhere love Raffi's songs.

Raffi, one of the world's most well-known children's performers, was raised in Toronto. Celine Dion, a popular modern singer, was born in Quebec.

Farley Mowat, an author and **naturalist**, was born in the city of Ottawa. Many of his books are about his life in Canada. Lucy Maud Montgomery, the author of the beloved Anne of Green Gables series, was born on Prince Edward Island. Today, fans still tour her home.

Fishers on these boats off Nova Scotia are heading out hoping for a good day's catch.

Jobs

Canadians hold a variety of jobs. Most work in banks, government, schools, hospitals, and other service-related fields.

Fishing and timber are also big industries. Large catches of salmon, herring, perch, and other fish come to the docks daily. Workers help transport the fish to restaurants and sometimes even all the way to different countries.

Keepsakes

Easter is a very popular holiday in Canada and is often celebrated for four days. Many families near the city of Winnipeg originally came from **Ukraine**. These families have a special Easter tradition. They paint delicate, colorful designs on eggs. They believe doing this will bring them health and happiness.

For many years, the Inuit have carved figures on soft, slippery stone called soapstone. They once carved tools out of this stone. Today, however, soapstone carvings are more commonly seen as artwork.

The designs on Ukrainian Easter eggs are intricate and beautiful.

Pysankas

(pie-SAN-kas) are Ukrainian Easter eggs.

Inuit soapstone carving of a polar bear

17

Land

Tombstone Valley in the Yukon is beautiful in any season, but especially when burnished with autumn colors.

Canada is very big! It is the second-largest country in the world.

A tranquil farm on Prince Edward Island

The ten provinces in Canada range from tiny Prince Edward Island to huge Quebec. The territories are divided up into the Northwest Territories, Nunavut, and the Yukon. There are forests, plains, mountains, and plenty of rivers and lakes.

Much of northern Canada is tundra. The tundra is so cold that the ground never really thaws. This is called **permafrost**. Few plants grow on the tundra. It is mostly a land of mosses and lichens.

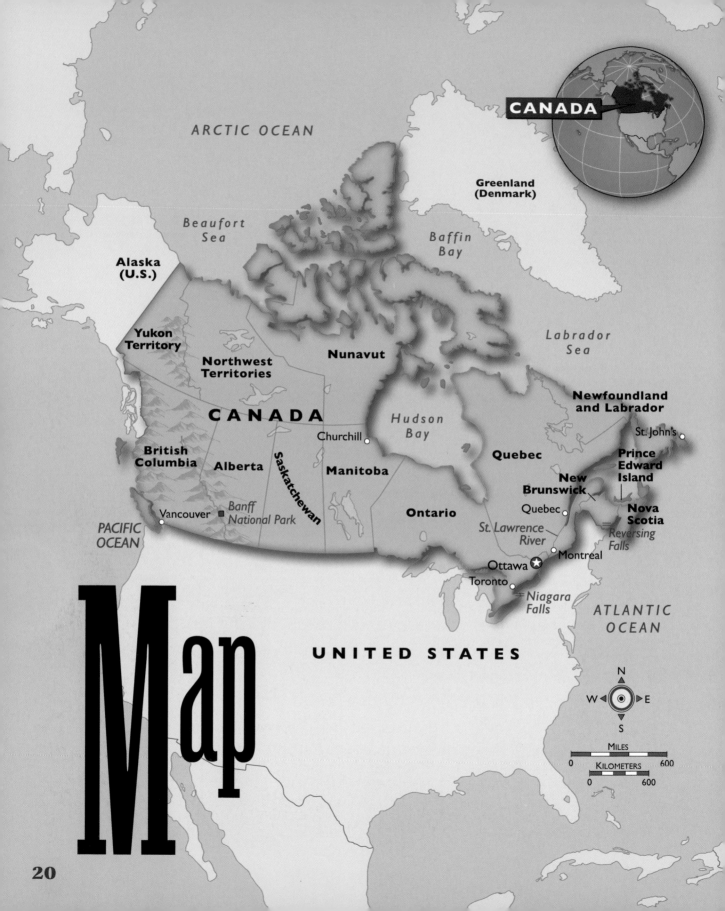

CANADA

ARCTIC OCEAN

Greenland
(Denmark)

*Beaufort
Sea*

*Baffin
Bay*

Alaska
(U.S.)

Yukon
Territory

Northwest
Territories

Nunavut

*Labrador
Sea*

CANADA

Newfoundland
and Labrador

British
Columbia

Alberta

Saskatchewan

Manitoba

Churchill

*Hudson
Bay*

Quebec

St. John's

Prince
Edward
Island

New
Brunswick

Nova
Scotia

Vancouver

*Banff
National Park*

Ontario

Quebec

*Reversing
Falls*

PACIFIC
OCEAN

*St. Lawrence
River*

Montreal

Ottawa

Toronto

*Niagara
Falls*

ATLANTIC
OCEAN

UNITED STATES

Map

N
W · E
S

MILES
0   600

KILOMETERS
0   600

ation

The Canadian flag has changed over time. For almost 350 years, it was the same as the United Kingdom's flag. It was not until 1965 that the current flag came into being.

Designed by a man named Dr. George Stanley, this flag has two red stripes, one on each end. Between them is a white stripe with a red maple leaf in the middle. The maple leaf is the national symbol of Canada. Red and white have been Canada's colors since 1921.

Maple leaves are a national symbol in Canada.

Only in Canada

Everywhere you look in Canada, you can spot the image of a maple leaf. And no wonder!

**Water flows backward twice each day at
the fantastic Reversing Falls at Saint John.**

There are only thirteen types of maple trees in North America, and
ten of those grow in Canada. At least one type of maple tree grows in
every province.

One of Canada's most amazing sights may be found in the province
of New Brunswick. The waterfalls there are lovely—but they also do
something remarkable. Twice a day, at high tide, the water level gets so
high that the water has to go backward! The Reversing Falls at Saint John
are famous around the world.

People

Inuusiq

(ee-new-oo-sik)
means "way of life" in Inuit.

The Inuit were among the first people to make Canada their home. Today, many native Canadian Inuit still live in the Arctic regions of Canada. In 1999, they were given their own territory, called Nunavut, which means "our land." Nunavut is a place where the Inuit can respect and honor their unique culture and traditions.

Gateway to Chinatown in Victoria, British Columbia

Canada has more than 600,000 Native Americans. They are sometimes called the First Nations people.

Many Canadians are of British descent, but immigrants from other parts of the world have also settled here. Chinese people live in areas such as Victoria's Chinatown. People of Scottish descent often are found in Nova Scotia, while Quebec is home to many French families.

This crossing guard in Quebec tells people to stop in both French and English.

Look for the surprise inside this birthday cake!

Question What is inside your birthday cake?

Eating a piece of birthday cake is always fun, but in Canada, it can be especially exciting. Many cakes have a hidden surprise tucked between the layers. It may be a toy or a foil-covered piece of candy. Whoever finds the surprise is honored and gets to go first for all of the party games.

Inside Notre-Dame Basilica

Native American dancer

In Canada, everyone is free to choose what they believe. Almost half of the people are Roman Catholic, and they have many churches such as the Notre-Dame Basilica in Montreal.

Other diverse faiths can be found throughout Canada. Asian immigrants introduced religions such as Buddhism. Mennonites and Jews came from Russia, and Presbyterians came from Scotland. Native Americans continue to worship using traditional ceremonies.

Religion

Ice hockey is Canada's favorite sport.

School & Sports

Education in Canada is much like it is in the United States. Some children in the far north do not live close enough to attend school. Instead, they may be homeschooled, taught through classes on the computer, or enrolled in **correspondence classes.**

Canadians invented the game of hockey in 1875, and more than one hundred years later it is still the country's favorite sport. Children learn to ice-skate at a very young age. There are many indoor and outdoor rinks. During the winter, people of all ages can be found playing on frozen ponds.

Attentive first-graders

Ferries are a familiar sight on Canada's rivers and lakes.

Skidoo

(SKID-oo)
is a popular name
for snowmobile.

Transportation

Canada has an excellent system of highways and railroads. The Trans-Canada Highway stretches from the Atlantic Ocean all the way to the Pacific. It is the longest national highway in the world!

Ferries and other boats carry people and goods across Canada's many lakes and rivers. Bush planes haul passengers and supplies to northern Canada, where there are few roads. Many of these planes are specially designed to land on water.

In 1922, a Canadian named Armand Bombardier invented the snowmobile. In winter, snowmobiles travel where cars and trucks can't!

Trees grow out of enormous rock formations along the coast of New Brunswick.

Unusual Places

If you visit New Brunswick's Flowerpot Rocks when the tide is in, you may be disappointed. As you look across the water, all you'll see are a lot of little islands with trees growing on top. But if you wait until the tide goes out, you'll observe something amazing. The trees are actually growing on red rocks that are 50 feet (15 m) tall and look a lot like flowerpots!

Banff National Park offers breathtaking vistas wherever you look.

Visiting the Country

For tourists who like the outdoors, one of the best stops in Canada is Alberta's Banff National Park. With more than 2,500 square miles (6,500 sq kilometers) to explore, visitors can go hiking, tour caves, and look for wolves, elk, caribou, and grizzly bears.

Would you prefer a trip to the West Edmonton Mall? Featuring more than eight hundred stores, it also has the largest indoor lake in the world and the largest indoor triple-loop roller coaster!

An old Hudson's Bay trading post on the vast Canadian prairie

Window to the Past

Today, Inuit families still shop at Hudson's Bay Company stores.

In 1670, England set up a trading company in Canada called Hudson's Bay Company. England hoped to compete against the French trading posts that were popping up along the Saint Lawrence River and the Great Lakes. The company was a success, trading in furs all around Hudson Bay and west to the Pacific Ocean.

Three hundred years later, their success continues. Hudson's Bay department stores can still be found throughout Canada.

X-tra Special Things

A Maid of the Mist tourist boat (bottom right) carries sightseers at Niagara Falls (top).

The aurora borealis, or northern lights

Northern pitcher plant

On the border between Ontario and New York is one of the greatest natural wonders of the world, Niagara Falls. For more than a century, Niagara has generated electricity for parts of Ontario and New York. Tourists enjoy riding the Maid of the Mist boats that get close to the roaring waterfalls.

One of Canada's most unusual plants is the pitcher plant, a plant that can trap and digest insects. Because this plant grows in poor soil, it needs extra **nutrients**. Fortunately, its shiny pink and rose blossoms attract bugs, spiders, and even frogs. They stop for a look and tumble into the bottom of the slippery, bowl-shaped plant. An **enzyme** dissolves them and creates the perfect meal.

High above the country is another wonder. It's the aurora borealis, or northern lights. Filling the skies with flickering, dancing colors, they are the result of solar particles hitting Earth's atmosphere.

Yearly Festivals

In the eastern provinces, spring is full of maple syrup festivals. Both children and adults look forward to this sweet time!

People gather in Gatineau every summer for the annual hot air balloon festival. In addition to watching the colorful balloon launches, visitors enjoy fireworks displays and live music.

A patriotic Canadian celebrating Canada Day

Fireworks light up Ottawa's Parliament buildings on Canada Day.

Canada Day is observed throughout the country on July 1. On this day in 1867, Canadian provinces were united and Great Britain gave the Canadian people permission to govern themselves. Cities mark the day with parades, picnics, parties, and fireworks.

Zipper

The man credited with creating the slide fastener, or zipper, was Canadian-raised Dr. Gideon Sundback. Although others had worked on the idea before him, Dr. Sundback was the first to improve and sell zippers. His Lightning Fastener Company was based out of Saint Catherine's, Ontario.

What would the world be like without zippers?

■ Canadian and English Words

correspondence classes classes that are conducted through lesson plans and exercises that are mailed back and forth between a teacher and students

enzyme a protein that is made by living creatures and works like a chemical

kilts pleated, plaid skirts that reach to the knees and are worn by some Scottish men

kimonos loose robes or gowns tied with a belt and worn by people from Japan

lichens fungus and an alga that grow together on rocks or trees and that resemble moss

migrate to move from one place to another

monarch a ruler, such as a king or queen, who often inherits his or her position

naturalist a person who knows a great deal about animals or plants

nutrients things needed by people, animals, and plants to stay strong and healthy

permafrost an area so cold that the ground never thaws

provinces the main divisions of a country

territories large areas of land or regions

tundra a huge, treeless plain in Arctic regions

Ukraine a country in Eastern Europe

■ Let's Explore More

Canada: A MyReportLinks.com Book by Pat McCarthy, Enslow Publishers, 2004

Canada: Many Cultures, One World by Kay Melchisedech Olson, Blue Earth Books, 2004

Canada by Shirley W. Gray, Compass Point Books, 2000

Websites

http://www.gov.nu.ca/Nunavut/
This site provides information about the newest territory in Canada, dedicated to the heritage and traditions of the Inuit.

http://www.niagarafallslive.com/Facts_about_Niagara_Falls.htm
This site offers information on Niagara Falls and its history. See wonderful color pictures of the falls in action!

http://www.worldalmanacforkids.com/explore/nations/canada.html
This huge site offers all the facts you'd like to know about Canada, from history to current statistics.

Index

Italic page numbers indicate illustrations.

Meet the Author

TAMRA ORR is a full-time author living in Portland, Oregon. She has written fifty books for children and families. Many of her books have been about different places all over the planet—including *Slovenia, Turkey,* and *Taiwan* for Scholastic, and *New Jersey, Colorado, Barbados,* and *Windward Islands* for several other publishers. In 2004, one of her books won the New York Public Library's Best Nonfiction Book for Teens award. In addition to books, Orr writes multiple articles for magazines and also works for several national standardized testing companies.

Orr graduated from Ball State University in Muncie, Indiana, and in the fall of 2001, she and her husband and four children (ages nine to twenty-one) moved across the country from Indiana to Oregon. She visits Canada more often now because she lives so close. Orr vaguely remembers riding the *Maid of the Mist* when she was six and feeling the spray of the waterfalls on her face.